EXPLORE
my world

Dolphins

Becky Baines

NATIONAL
GEOGRAPHIC
KiDS

WASHINGTON, D.C.

Splash!

Diving into blue ocean waters, a bottlenose dolphin gracefully glides under waves and then leaps high in the air!

Dolphins live in family groups. Do you see one, two, three, four? Sometimes there are even more!

Living in a group helps dolphins find food and stay safe. Dolphins must watch out for sharp shark teeth, fishing nets, and boats that buzz by.

In deep ocean waters, groups of dolphins might get together to form a school. A school can have hundreds of dolphins in it! But in shallow water you are more likely to see fewer than 12 dolphins together.

Hello!

Did you know
that dolphins talk?
Instead of words,
they make sounds like
clicks, squawks, and whistles.
Each dolphin has its own
whistle, just like you have your
own name.

A baby dolphin even knows the
sound of its mom's call.

Chow Time!

What's your favorite food?

shrimp

Dolphins dine on fast fish and slimy squid, crawling crabs, and squirmy shrimp. But it can be hard to see in the dark ocean. How do dolphins find food?

squid

fish

A dolphin "sees" with sound. As it swims along, the dolphin makes a clicking noise. When the noise hits something in the dolphin's path, the sound bounces back.

That tells the dolphin the size, shape, and speed of its dinner … and right where to find it!

Watch out for those pincers!

crab

What is this dolphin eating for lunch?

Gulp!

Dolphins hunting together swim round and round. They crowd a school of fish into a tight little bunch. Then they take turns swooping in, mouths open for a snack.

Dolphin teeth are shaped like upside-down ice-cream cones. They are great for grabbing!

A dolphin's body is made for swimming. They have flippers that help them stop, start, and turn.

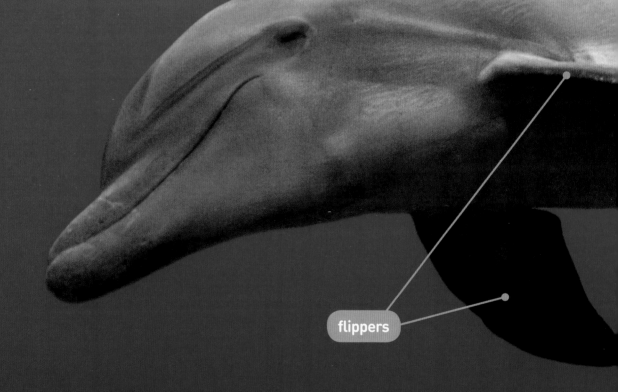

flippers

dorsal fin

tail

They have a strong tail that goes up and down, pushing them forward, fast. They have a big dorsal fin that keeps them swimming straight.

Marine Mammals

Dolphins are mammals—just like you!

Mammals are warm-blooded. A dolphin's body stays at a comfy 97°F.

Your normal body temperature is a warm 98.6°F.

Mammals have backbones. A dolphin's backbone bends so it can move its powerful tail.

Mammals have hair. Dolphin babies have hair on their noses!

Baby mammals drink their mom's milk. Dolphin babies need lots of milk to grow big and strong.

Do you have a tail?

What did you eat when you were a baby?

MILK

Can you touch your backbone?

Oh baby!

A baby dolphin, called a calf, is born just under the surface of the water. It is about the same size as a six-year-old boy or girl.

An adult dolphin takes a newborn calf up to the surface for a big breath of air. The calf pops out of the water and breathes through a hole in the top of its head.

The calf starts to swim right after it is born.

Grown-up dolphins have a layer of fat called blubber that keeps them warm, but calves don't. They keep warm by keeping up! Lots of mammals move around to stay warm.

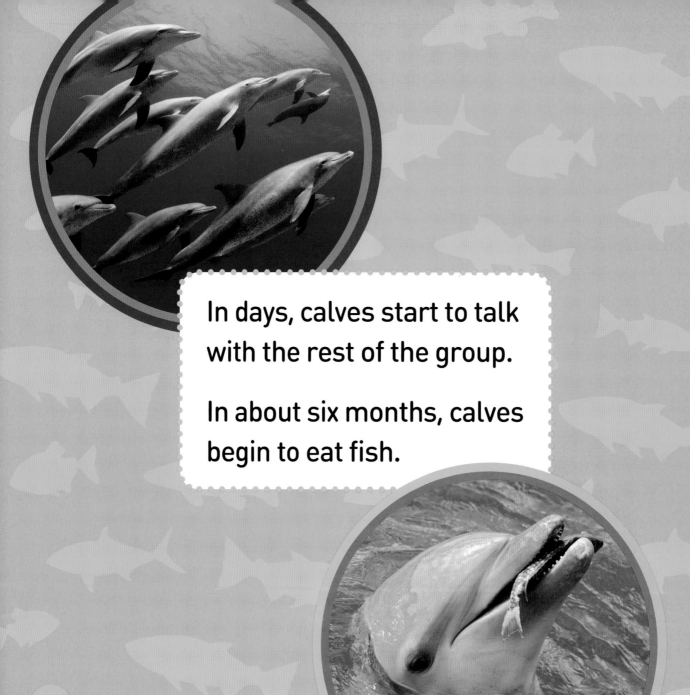

In days, calves start to talk with the rest of the group.

In about six months, calves begin to eat fish.

For about three years, a calf stays with its mother. When a dolphin is around six years old, it is all grown up.

Playtime!

Being a dolphin isn't all hard work. They enjoy fun and games!

Dolphins ride waves. *Yippee!*
They blow bubbles. *Boing!*
They leap high in the air.
Whee!

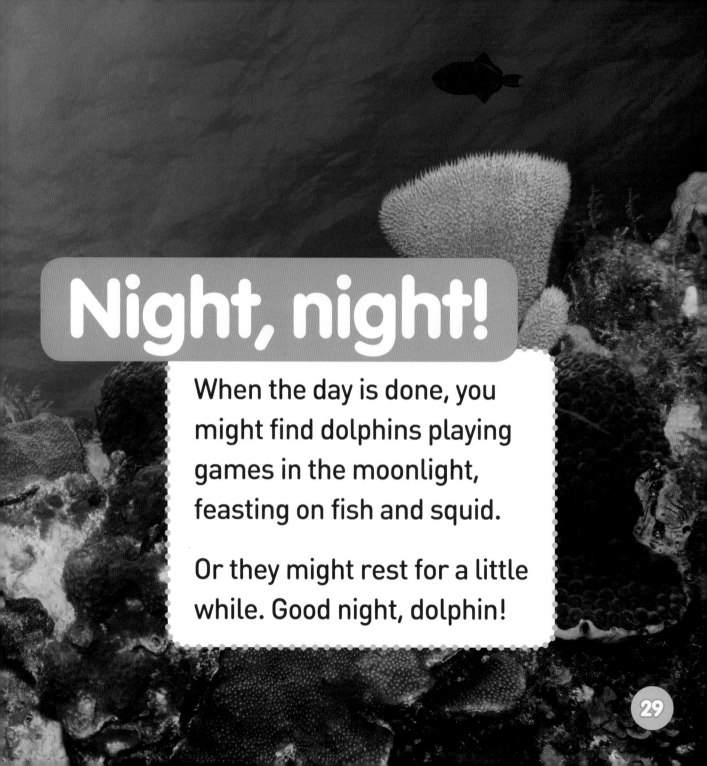

Night, night!

When the day is done, you might find dolphins playing games in the moonlight, feasting on fish and squid.

Or they might rest for a little while. Good night, dolphin!

Different Dolphins

bottlenose dolphin

orca

There are 43 different species, or kinds, of dolphins. The bottlenose dolphin is the most famous. These mammals live in oceans around the world. Some even live in rivers and lakes. If you ever go dolphin-watching, here are a few species you might meet.

dusky dolphin

spinner dolphin

Amazon river dolphin

spotted dolphin

rough-toothed dolphin

For Ellie Boo

National Geographic supports K–12 educators with ELA Common Core Resources. Visit natgeoed.org/commoncore for more information.

The publisher gratefully acknowledges Bruno Diaz Lopez, Chief Biologist and Director, Bottlenose Dolphin Research Institute, Pontevedra, Spain, for his expert review of the book.

STAFF FOR THIS BOOK

Catherine Hughes, *Executive Editor, Preschool Content*
Amanda Larsen, *Art Director and Designer*
Christina Ascani, *Photo Editor*
Paige Towler, *Editorial Assistant*
Sanjida Rashid and Rachel Kenny, *Design Production Assistants*
Tammi Colleary-Loach, *Rights Clearance Manager*
Michael Cassady and Mari Robinson, *Rights Clearance Specialists*
Grace Hill, *Managing Editor*
Joan Gossett, *Senior Production Editor*
Lewis R. Bassford, *Production Manager*
George Bounelis, *Manager, Production Services*
Susan Borke, *Legal and Business Affairs*

PHOTOGRAPHY CREDITS

Cover: tubuceo/Shutterstock; 1 (CTR), Wyland/SeaPics.com; 2-3 (CTR), Roland Seitre/Minden Pictures/Corbis; 4-5 (CTR), Brandon Cole; 6 (CTR), Minden Pictures/Getty Images; 7 (BACKGROUND), TSHOOTER/Shutterstock; 7 (UP RT), Doug Perrine/SeaPics.com; 7 (LO LE), Evlakhov/Shutterstock; 8-9 (CTR), Petra Wegner/Alamy; 10 (CTR), Universal Images Group/Getty Images; 11 (UP RT), Augusto Stanzani/ARDEA; 12 (UP RT), Jeff Rotman/Getty Images; 12 (LO LE), schankz/Shutterstock; 12 (LO RT), seksan wangjaisuk/Shutterstock; 12 (CTR LE), Weerachai Khamfu/Shutterstock; 13 (UP RT), chungking/Shutterstock; 13 (LO RT), Dickie Duckett/Minden Pictures; 14 (CTR), Doug Perrine/Alamy; 15 (CTR), Universal Images Group/Getty Images; 16-17 (CTR), Doug Perrine/SeaPics.com; 18 (LO LE), Alexey Tkachenko/Getty Images; 18 (UP RT), Francois Gohier/VWPics/Alamy; 18 (LO RT), Denniro/Shutterstock; 19 (LO CTR), Barry B. Brown/wildhorizons.com; 19 (UP RT), DmitriMaruta/Shutterstock; 19 (CTR RT), Hurst Photo/Shutterstock; 20 (BACKGROUND), yyang/Shutterstock; 20 (UP LE), Augusto Satanzini/ARDEA; 21 (CTR), Tim Davis/Corbis; 22-23 (CTR LE), Universal Images Group/Getty Images; 24 (UP LE), Natalia Pryanish-nikova/Alamy; 24 (LO RT), Nature/UIG/Getty Images; 25 (CTR), Universal Images Group/Getty Images; 26 (CTR), Masa Ushioda/SeaPics.com; 27 (UP LE), Stone/Getty Images; 27 (LO RT), Fco. Javier Gutiérrez/fotostock/Spain S.L./Corbis; 28-29 (CTR), Panoramic Images/Getty Images; 30 (LO LE), Martin Ruegner/Getty Images; 30 (UP RT), Natali Glado/Shutterstock; 31 (CTR LE), Kevin Schafer/Minden Pictures/Corbis; 31 (UP LE), Todd Pusser/SeaPics.com; 31 (LO LE), Andy Murch/SeaPics.com; 31 (CTR RT), Jody Watt/Design Pics/Corbis; 31 (LO RT), Matt9122/Shutterstock; 32 (LO LE), Augusto Stanzini/ARDEA

Library of Congress Cataloging-in-Publication Data

Baines, Rebecca, author.
 Dolphins / by Becky Baines.
    pages cm. — (Explore my world)
 Audience: Ages 3-7
 ISBN 978-1-4263-2318-8 (pbk. : alk. paper) — ISBN 978-1-4263-2319-5 (library binding : alk. paper)
 1. Dolphins—Juvenile literature. I. National Geographic Society (U.S.) II. Title. III. Series: Explore my world.
 QL737.C432B355 2016
 599.53—dc23
                                        2015027842

Printed in Hong Kong
15/THK/1